INSIDE THE WORLD OF SPORTS

GOLF

INSIDE THE WORLD OF SPORTS

AUTO RACING

BASEBALL

BASKETBALL

EXTREME SPORTS

FOOTBALL

GOLF

GYMNASTICS

ICE HOCKEY

LACROSSE

SOCCER

TENNIS

TRACK & FIELD

WRESTLING

INSIDE THE WORLD OF SPORTS

GOLF

by Andrew Luke

MC MASON CREST

Mason Crest
450 Parkway Drive, Suite D
Broomall, Pennsylvania 19008
(866) MCP-BOOK (toll free)

First printing
9 8 7 6 5 4 3 2

Names: Luke, Andrew, author.
Title: Golf / Andrew Luke.
Description: Broomall, Pennsylvania : Mason Crest, [2017] | Series: Inside
  the world of sports | Includes index.
Identifiers: LCCN 2015046234 (print) | LCCN 2016015608 (ebook) | ISBN
  9781422234617 (hardback) | ISBN 9781422234556 (series) | ISBN
  9781422284230 (ebook) | ISBN 9781422284230 (eBook)
Subjects: LCSH: Golf--History.
Classification: LCC GV963 .L85 2017 (print) | LCC GV963 (ebook) | DDC
  796.35209--dc23
LC record available at https://lccn.loc.gov/2015046234

QR CODES AND LINKS TO THIRD-PARTY CONTENT

CONTENTS

KEY ICONS TO LOOK FOR:

Words to understand: These words with their easy-to-understand definitions will increase the reader's understanding of the text while building vocabulary skills.

Educational Videos: Readers can view videos by scanning our QR codes, providing them with additional educational content to supplement the text. Examples include news coverage, moments in history, speeches, iconic sports moments and much more!

Text-dependent questions: These questions send the reader back to the text for more careful attention to the evidence presented there.

Research projects: Readers are pointed toward areas of further inquiry connected to each chapter. Suggestions are provided for projects that encourage deeper research and analysis.

The FedEx Cup is the trophy awarded to the winner of the PGA's year-end, four-tournament playoff. The playoff system was instituted for the 2007 season. The playoff series and the trophy bear the name of the event's primary sponsor, although each of the four tournaments has separate, individual sponsors. Players qualify for the playoff by accruing FedEx Cup points throughout the season. The top 150 point leaders qualify for the first tournament, and that is narrowed to 100 for the second event, 70 for the third, and just 30 for the final event, the Tour Championship tournament.

CHAPTER 1

GOLF'S GREATEST MOMENTS

Even the most devoted supporters will admit that golf can be a maddening, frustrating game. For most of us, it takes hours of practice and years of repetition to begin to get a handle on getting that little white ball to travel in a straight line with any consistency.

Keep your left arm straight. Keep your head still. Don't overswing. Swing with your shoulders, not your hands. These are just some of the tips both new and seasoned golfers try to implement in search of that most elusive element—the consistent golf swing.

The swing is just half of the battle. Once you get that ball near the hole, the other of golf's twin beasts rears its head—putting. Stand with your feet hip-distance apart. Play the ball forward in your stance. Grip the club lightly but firmly. Accelerate the club head through your point of balance. Variations on these tips have consumed countless hours on practice greens around the world for centuries.

Discerning which advice or combination of tips will produce a desirable result has caused many an average golfer to destroy a hostile driver or a defiant putter. As U.S. President Woodrow Wilson once famously said, "Golf is a game in which one endeavors to control a ball with implements ill adapted for the purpose."

But then, every 18 to 36 holes or so, it happens. That one swing produces a majestic drive that splits the fairway up the middle. That one putt from the fringe meanders its way to the bottom of the cup from a most unlikely distance. That one shot keeps us coming back.

It is the knowledge of just how difficult mastery of the game truly is that heightens the appreciation for those that make it look so effortless in the most challenging conditions. This is especially so when the stakes are at their highest, and the greatest golfers in the game execute plays that are so unlikely, so unimaginable, and so thrilling that they represent the greatest moments in the sport.

The Double Eagle

When Gene Sarazen played the Masters in 1935, he was already an established golf star. The tournament itself, however, was not. The Masters had debuted the year before and did not have the same status in the sport as the U.S. and British Opens. On the 15th hole in the fourth round, Sarazen changed that forever.

Sarazen trailed clubhouse leader Craig Wood by three shots as he teed off at the par-5 15th hole, meaning he needed at least three birdies over the last four holes to force a play-off. He hit a 265-yard drive down the right side, leaving 230 yards to the green. Sarazen selected a 4 wood for his second shot and let loose with a low blast that bounced once onto the green then once more before starting its roll toward the cup and infamy. The gallery erupted as it went in. Sarazen tied the tournament with one swing and went on to win in a play-off.

Miracle at Merion

By 1950, the U.S. Open was a major sporting event on the men's side, having been contested since 1895. The 1950 edition was held at Merion Golf Club near Philadelphia. Entering the final round, 1948 champion Ben Hogan trailed Lloyd Mangrum by two strokes. That Hogan was in contention at all was remarkable for the fact that he was still recovering from a serious car accident in 1949. Hogan suffered breaks to his ribs, collarbone, pelvis, and ankle. Doctors said he would be lucky to walk again.

For Hogan to even be playing, much less contending at the U.S. Open just over a year later was miraculous. Playing on painful legs that were still bandaged, Hogan famously saved par on the 18th hole with a terrific 1-iron shot. Hy Peskin's photo of the shot is one of the most famous in the sport. The shot helped Hogan get into an 18-hole playoff, which he won easily.

Palmer's Comeback

Ten years later, the U.S. Open was contested at Cherry Hills Country Club near Denver, Colorado, and was again the setting for another achievement by one of the sport's greats. Arnold Palmer entered the 1960 tournament having already won the Masters that season. He would go on to be named the 1960 Professional Golf Association (PGA) Player of the Year, and the U.S. Open was a large reason why.

The first three rounds had not gone well for Palmer, and he trailed Mike Souchak by seven shots entering the fourth round. Palmer started the round in spectacular fashion, however, driving the green on the first hole. He birdied the first four holes and six of the first seven. Palmer held on to shoot 65, a then-U.S. Open record six under par, and won by two strokes over Jack Nicklaus, who played as a 22-year-old amateur. Souchak shot a disastrous 75. The win represents the greatest comeback in U.S. Open history.

The Golden Bear Wins His Sixth

At the 1986 Masters, Nicklaus was 46 and in the twilight of his brilliant career. He was the winner of a record 17 major titles but had not won a major in six years, the longest such span in his career. It looked as though the drought would continue when round four started with Nicklaus four shots behind leader Greg Norman. Thirteen other golfers were either tied with or ahead of him.

None of those other golfers had a back nine like Nicklaus did that Sunday. He shot –1 on the front nine but then made three birdies and an eagle in the next six holes. When he walked onto the 17th green to survey another birdie putt, he was at –8, tied with Seve Ballesteros and Tom Kite. The image of Nicklaus raising his putter as the 11-footer dropped in to give him the lead in an eventual winning round of 65 is one of golf's most iconic.

Mize's Masterful Chip

The following year, the drama at the Masters was provided by a much less celebrated player. In 1987, Larry Mize was a six-year pro with just a single tour win under his belt. But he scratched and clawed his way into a play-off on Sunday with Ballesteros and Norman, the world's top two players at the time.

It was a sudden-death play off, and Ballesteros shockingly three-putted the first playoff hole, the 10th, and was eliminated. That left current British Open champion Norman, the powerful Australian nicknamed "The Great White Shark," and Mize, the Augusta, Georgia, native with little major championship experience. On the 11th hole, Norman landed his second shot on the edge of the green. Mize was not as good, missing the putting surface altogether and ending up 140 feet (42.7 m) away. But Mize was magical with his next shot, a chip for the ages that bounced twice before rolling up onto the green and in for the win.

"The Greatest Performance in Golf History"

The 1986 and 1987 Masters featured great performances by their champions but not as good as the one put in by 1997 champion Eldrick "Tiger" Woods. Woods made history that year by posting a course record 18 under 270 to win by 12 strokes. Jordan Spieth tied the record in 2015, but no one has ever matched the margin of victory. The win was significant because the private Augusta National Golf Club had only allowed black players since 1990, and a 21-year-old black player delivered what *Sports Illustrated* magazine called at the time "the greatest performance ever seen in a golf major."

Sports Illustrated would say almost the same thing about Woods three years later after the 2000 U.S. Open at Pebble Beach, California. Woods won that tournament by 15 shots, a record for any major. On its cover, *Sports Illustrated* proclaimed it "the greatest performance in golf history." No one has come close to matching it.

Birdie for Birdie

Forty-five years after Arnold Palmer made his huge comeback in the U.S. Open at Cherry Hills Country Club, the venue was host to the 2005 U.S. Women's Open. The tournament is best remembered for a shot made by a player with a perfect golf name. South Korean Birdie Kim was tied for the lead as she played the 18th and final hole of the final round. The 18th was the toughest hole on the course, yielding just three birdies total for the tournament.

Who better to notch the fourth than someone named Birdie Kim? A birdie seemed unlikely for Kim as her second shot found a greenside bunker. Undeterred, she calmly stepped down into the sand, settled behind the ball, and lifted it out. The shot landed softly and rolled unwaveringly into the cup to give Kim her only Ladies Professional Golf Association (LPGA) win.

Bubba Golf

Gerry "Bubba" Watson, Jr. is known for making tough shots in difficult situations. On the tour, this ability is called "Bubba golf", and never was it on finer display than in the sudden-death playoff at the 2012 Masters. Watson and South Africa's Louis Oosthuizen were tied after 72 holes, plus one sudden-death hole. On the second sudden-death hole, the par-4 10th, both men drove their tee shots to the right.

Oosthuizen ended up in the rough, but Watson ended up deep in the woods. Resting among the pine needles, Watson's ball was 164 yards (150 m) from the green, but several trees blocked any direct shot at the flagstick. So Watson played a little Bubba golf, hitting a spectacular hook shot that curved 40 yards (36.6 m) and came to rest on the green, just 15 feet (4.6 m) from the hole. He made par, good enough to win his first major.

"The MacDonald boys playing golf"
by Jeremiah Davison, 18th century

Words to Understand:

caddy: a player's assistant who carries the clubs and gives advice on how to play the hole

featheries: early golf balls made with leather sack stuffed with boiled feathers.

trajectory: the curve of an object in flight

indelible: that which cannot be eliminated, forgotten, or changed.

CHAPTER 2

THE ORIGINS OF GOLF

Scotland is considered to be the birthplace of the modern-day version of the game of golf. The high bluffs of the country's eastern coastline provided natural mounds and ridges to challenge those who had decided it was great fun to hit rocks with wooden clubs from one point to another. The game was so popular in 15th-century Scotland that King James II banned it because it was distracting men from practicing their archery. With war a constant threat in the late Middle Ages, the king could not abide such a distraction.

The famous Swilcan Bridge on the 18th hole of the Old Course, St. Andrews Links, in Scotland.

THE ROYAL AND ANCIENT GAME

The ban was ironic in that the game was most popular in the Scottish and English royal houses. Mary, Queen of Scots, famously mourned by playing a round in 1567 following the death of her husband. The Duke of York, who would go on to become King James III, was one of the first to employ the use of a **caddy**.

By the 17th and 18th centuries, the game was extremely popular with the Scottish upper class, which organized into clubs to play the game. The year 1744 saw the Magistrates and Council of Edinburgh develop the first 13 official rules and regulations governing match play golf. The Society of St. Andrew's adopted the rules in 1754. In 1854, the society officially was renamed the Royal and Ancient Golf Club of St. Andrew's and became the recognized governing body of the game, developing and standardizing rules.

AN ORGANIZED SPORT

The first golf tournament took place in the western town of Prestwick, Scotland, in 1860. When it evolved in later years to be open to anyone who wanted to play, it became known as the Open Championship. The tournament was in a man-to-man match play format consisting of three rounds of 12 holes each. When stroke play developed, St. Andrew's arbitrarily set the number of holes per round at 18, which was universally adopted as the standard.

Since this first effort at organization in the 19th century, the core rules of the sport have not changed significantly. The biggest changes in the sport of golf have been and continue to be in the tools and equipment employed to play it.

William Inglis, c 1712–1792, surgeon and captain of the Honourable Company of Edinburgh Golfers.

LONGER BALLS

Wood was the early material of choice for both clubs and balls. The balls evolved first, with wood being replaced by a leather sack stuffed with boiled feathers. These **featheries** were popular in the first half of the 19th century, until balls formed from Malaysian tree sap (a substance called gutta percha) replaced them in popularity in 1848. Gutty balls had a driving distance of 225 yards (205.7 m), about 50 yards (45.7 m) better than that of featheries. These drives took place off of small mounds of sand until tees were invented in Scotland in 1889.

Antique wooden driver and putter.

American contributions to the game came shortly after this. A group of transplanted Scots led by Robert Lockhart and John Reid started playing the game near New York City in the 1880s. Reid founded the six-hole St. Andrew's Golf Club in Yonkers in 1888, and the game exploded. In 1895, the *New York Times* reported, "In the history of American field sports there can be found no outdoor pastime that developed and attained such popularity in uch a relatively short period of time." In 1898, American Coburn Haskell invented the rubber-cored ball, around which was wound rubber thread, all encased in a gutta percha or balata cover. Dimples were added to the cover in the early 1900s to help control **trajectory**, flight, and spin.

STRONGER CLUBS

Golf club technology lagged behind. No one even thought of a better way to carry them around until the golf bag was invented in 1860. Before that, they were just bundled together, gripped by the handles, and perched on the shoulder of the player or caddy. In 1910, steel shafts replaced the traditional hand-carved wood. Because steel could be mass-produced, making clubs became much more efficient and thus much cheaper.

TRANSATLANTIC APPEAL

In 1932 the current 1.62-ounce (45.9 g), 1.68-inch (4.3 cm) diameter ball became the standard for the sport, and by 1939, the limit of 14 total clubs per player was imposed. Both of these developments were initiated in America, which quickly became the leader in improvements to the game.

The love and devotion for golf (the word derived from old English for *club*) nurtured by the Scots over the centuries, however, are the reasons for the sport's existence and popularity today.

A PROMINENT PIONEER

One Scot in particular made an **indelible** mark on the game. In the early 1800s, Allan Robertson was the links keeper at St. Andrew's. Robertson was locally renowned for his skill on the links, a master of control and accuracy.

Robertson famously hired 14-year-old Tom Morris as his apprentice in 1835. He taught Morris the game, and the two were unbeatable as a team in challenge matches. Morris eventually took over as greenkeeper, club maker, ball maker, golf instructor, and course designer at St. Andrew's, where he helped organize the Open Championship, winning three of the first five tournaments.

Allan Robertson, Pioneer Professional Golfer at St. Andrews, Scotland, about 1850

Old Tom Morris addressing the ball, about 1905

Text-Dependent Questions:

1. What country is considered to be the birthplace of the modern-day version of the game of golf?

2. What kind of material were the earliest golf clubs and balls made out of?

3. What is the name of Allan Robertson's apprentice who eventually helped to organize the Open Championship?

Research Project:

Compare how clubs and balls have changed over time. How is STEM (science, technology, engineering, and math) used in the design of today's modern equipment?

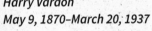

Harry Vardon
May 9, 1870–March 20, 1937

Words to Understand:

triumvirate: any group or set of three

forefront: a position of great importance or prominence

argyle: a diamond-shaped pattern of two or more colors, used in knitting socks, sweaters, etc.

CHAPTER

THE MEN WHO GREW THE GAME

The love of golf was fostered in Scotland with great success, but Scotland's neighbors were slower to find similar enthusiasm for the game. In England the game was viewed as bizarre and as a strange pursuit as a hobby for a grown man.

THE GREAT TRIUMVIRATE

There were three players who were instrumental in making the game popular outside of Scotland and in Europe in particular. Harry Vardon was from England and could hit the ball straighter than anyone else. His swing was one of the most copied elements in all of golf, along with his grip. Vardon succeeded using a grip where the pinky of the right hand overlapped the index finger of the left. The grip is still used widely today. Vardon won six Open Championships between 1896 and 1914.

JAMES BRAID AND JOHN HENRY TAYLOR

James Braid won the Open Championship five times between 1901 and 1910. The Scotsman was not only a superb player known for power but also a club maker and golf course builder, designing more than 100 courses in his career.

John Henry Taylor was the third of the men known as "the Great **Triumvirate**." He won the Open Championship five times between 1894 and 1913. Following his impressive career, Taylor was a founder of the British PGA and helped spur the creation of more public courses in the UK.

Scottish golfer James Braid (1870–1950) playing at the Open de France at Chantilly in 1913.

John Henry Taylor, English golfing great and winner of five Open Championships between 1894 and 1913.

23

Newport Country Club, founded in 1893, is a historic private golf club in Newport, Rhode Island, that hosted both the first U.S. Amateur Championship and the first U.S. Open in 1895.

Horace Rawlins was an English professional golfer who won the first U.S. Open Championship in 1895. With this victory, he became the first winner of a "major" outside the United Kingdom.

GOLF IN AMERICA

While Vardon, Braid, and Taylor were dominating the game in Scotland, in America, golf was getting more organized, and American ingenuity was driving innovation in the sport.

Six years after the St. Andrew's Golf Club was founded in Yonkers, the United States Golf Association (USGA) was formed in 1894, and the first U.S. Open tournament was held. The following year, a group of female golfers organized the first USGA Women's Amateur Championship. The USGA became the authority and controlling body for the sport in America and remains so today.

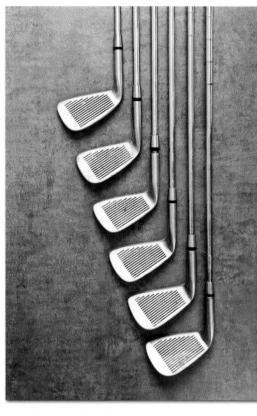

AMERICAN DIVERSITY

Not only did Americans develop the rubber-cored golf ball, but metal clubs were an American innovation as well. Dr. George Grant, a black dentist from Oswego, New York, held the first patent on a golf tee. American golf as run by the USGA has a history of being more inclusive than the team sports that also were becoming popular in this era.

In 1896, John Shippen, a black man who taught the game at the famous Shinnecock Golf Course on Long Island, registered to play in the U.S. Open, as did Native American Oscar Bunn. The other competitors, all white Americans, Britons, or Europeans, threatened to boycott the event if Shippen and Bunn were allowed to compete. USGA President Theodore Havermyer refused to be intimidated, promising the tournament would be held even if the two players in questions were the only competitors to tee off. The objectors gave in and played as scheduled.

FRANCIS OUIMET

The first American to bring golf to the **forefront** for the general American public was 20-year-old Boston native Francis Ouimet. In 1913, he was an amateur star playing in his first professional event, the U.S. Open. Two English players, former U.S. Open champion and five-time Open Championship winner Harry Vardon and Ted Ray, were considered the top two players in the world at the time. Ouimet matched them stroke for stroke, and when the tournament ended with the three tied and headed for an 18-hole playoff, Ouimet quickly became the talk of the country. The playoff drew the largest crowds seen to this point in American golf, and when Ouimet did the unthinkable by winning, golf as a mainstream U.S. sport was born.

Suddenly, all of America was looking to take up the game. Three years after Ouimet's win, so many amateur golfers turned pro that the PGA was formed in conjunction with its annual championship tournament. The number of registered golfers in the country tripled by 1923, and every U.S. city of any significant size had a public course, which had been extremely rare. Baggy knickers and **argyle** vests were all the rage from Boston to Boise.

INTERNATIONAL COMPETITION

Soon, what was once the undisputed domain of the British stars was no longer so. Associations from both sides of the pond agreed to organize competitions to be held every other year that pitted teams of players from Great Britain against American counterparts. Today, the three main competitions are the Ryder Cup, for male professionals, the Walker Cup, for male amateurs, and the Curtis Cup, for female amateurs.

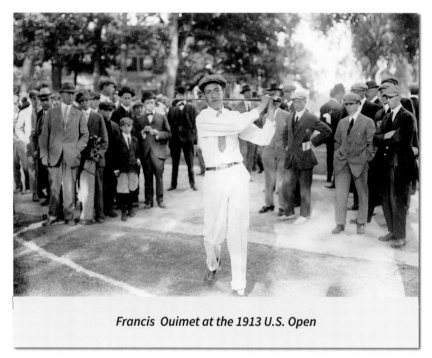

Francis Ouimet at the 1913 U.S. Open

Text-Dependent Questions:

1. Name the three players who were instrumental in making the game of golf popular outside of Scotland and in Europe in particular?

2. In what year was the USGA formed and the first U.S. Open tournament held?

3. Who is credited as the first American to bring golf to the forefront for the American public?

Research Project:

Read more about "the Great Triumvirate," and compare them to today's greatest players. How do the first three greats compare to today's modern stars?

Bobby Jones
(March 17, 1902–December 18, 1971)

Words to Understand:

amateur: a person who does something (such as a sport or hobby) for pleasure and not as a job

perpetuated: to cause to last indefinitely

flamboyant: having a very noticeable quality that attracts a lot of attention

CHAPTER 4

THE EARLY STARS

One of the best players to emerge in the aftermath of Francis Ouimet's U.S. Open triumph was an **amateur** from Atlanta, Georgia, named Bobby Jones. Jones was 11 when Ouimet pushed golf into the national spotlight and was already a prodigy, having taken up the game as a prescription to get stronger after chronic childhood illnesses. He was 21 when he won the U.S. Open in 1923.

Jones had one of the most successful amateur careers ever, winning all four major tournaments in 1930. He is rumored to have bet on himself to achieve this Grand Slam with English bookies, collecting $60,000. Amazingly, golf was a hobby for Jones, who never played professionally. A brilliant student, he earned a law degree in 1926 and quit golf to focus on his legal career in 1930. He stayed connected to the game, however, and was the founder and designer of Augusta National and the Masters.

Bobby Jones with Melvin A. Traylor

GOLF'S FASHION PLATE

With his slicked-back hair, baggy knickers, and two-toned shoes, Walter Hagan certainly made a statement with his **flamboyant** sense of style during his career. But he also made a statement with his clubs as well as he was one of the dominant players of his era.

Hagen was the opposite of Jones in that he embraced the professional aspect of the game wholeheartedly. Hagen was one of the first to make money from endorsing golf equipment, a staple of income for today's pros. He also made a lot of money playing exhibition matches, which paid him more than winning actual tournaments. Hagen played in all the big events, however, and in 1922 was the first American to win the Open Championship, by then commonly called the British Open.

The Golf World Champion Walter Hagen (left) and Horton Smith (right), at the International Golf Championship in Wannsee near Berlin, Germany 1929.

SLAMMIN' SAMMY

Hagen was known for his style along with his deadly putter, but in 1937, the year after Hagen's last PGA win, Sam Snead broke onto the tour sporting what might be the most iconic fashion piece in golf history. The Virginian sported a porkpie straw hat on the course, which he wore faithfully for more than 40

years. He also pioneered another now-famous look in golf—the green jacket. The tradition of the jacket being awarded to the Masters champion began with Snead's tournament win in 1949.

Stars of the 1920s and 1930s like Snead, Hagen, Jones, and Byron Nelson were products of the boom created by Francis Ouimet, and they **perpetuated** the sport's popularity with their outstanding play. There was a time when Jones was one of the top five best-known athletes in America, beside Babe Ruth, Jack Dempsey, Red Grange, and Bill Tilden. Golf had indeed arrived on American sports' main stage.

POSTWAR BOOM

The American economy was booming as the 1940s turned into the 1950s, and American passion for the game of golf boomed right along with it. At the forefront of the new crop of players helping to keep the game popular was Texan Ben Hogan.

Hogan developed a reputation for having one of the best swings the game has ever seen, and he practiced it relentlessly. Jack Nicklaus often said Hogan was the best ball striker he ever saw. His best season was 1953, when he won three majors. That was the most he could win that year, since the British Open and the PGA Championship were played at the same time (he won the British).

Ben Hogan is widely acknowledged to have been among the greatest ball strikers ever to have played golf.

31

THE BABE

One of the other great players of the era was also from Texas and perhaps the most influential player in the history of women's golf. Mildred "Babe" Didrikson was already famous long before she became serious about golf. Didrikson won two gold and one silver medal in track and field at the 1932 Summer Olympics in Los Angeles, California. She set a world record in winning the 80-meter (87.4 yard) hurdles and an Olympic record to win the javelin event. The silver medal came in the high jump.

A superb all-around athlete, Didrikson also excelled in volleyball, tennis, baseball, swimming, and basketball in high school. It was not surprising that when she turned to golf in 1935 that she succeeded there as well. That same year, she won the Texas Woman's Amateur Championship. Three years later, now known as Babe Zaharias after her marriage, she turned pro and was the first woman to compete in a men's event. She had a stellar golf career, but her biggest contribution was as co-founder of the LPGA. Determined to raise the profile of women's sports in general and golf in particular, she attracted the tour's first sponsors, and her celebrity kept it afloat in the early years.

Babe Didrickson excelled in several sports, including track and field and basketball. She took up golf at age 24 and became the greatest player of her era.

THE GOLDEN GOPHER

Zaharias's key co-founder of the LPGA was Minnesota native Patty Berg. Playing for the University of Minnesota Golden Gophers, she burst onto the golf scene when she made the final of the U.S. Women's Amateur in 1935. Berg turned pro in 1940 and won more major tournaments than any woman in history. She was the first president of the new LPGA in 1950.

Text-Dependent Questions:

1. Who is one of the first golfers to make money from endorsing golf equipment?

2. The tradition of the green jacket being awarded to the Masters champion began with a tournament win in 1949 by which golfer who regularly donned a green jacket?

3. Why was Mildred "Babe" Didrikson already famous long before she became serious about golf?

Research Project:

As noted, Hagen was one of the first to make money from endorsing golf equipment, a staple of income for today's pros. Take a closer look at the endorsements from today's golf stars. How much money do they make off the course by endorsing products? Which manufacturers pay the most? What kinds of responsibilities accompany an endorsement for the player in today's culture?

Charles Luther Sifford
(June 2, 1922–February 3, 2015)

Words to Understand:

beneficiaries: a person or organization that is helped by something; someone or something that benefits from something

telegenic: tending to look good or seem likable on television

prodigy: a young person who is unusually talented in some way

CHAPTER 5

THE GAME PROGRESSES

While women were making their mark in the sport and becoming more widely respected as players in the 1950s, the same could not be said for black players. The USGA, operators of the U.S. Open, allowed anyone to play, but reflective of the struggle for civil rights in the country as a whole, black players were banned from playing on the PGA Tour by a bylaw in its constitution that required all members to be of the Caucasian race. This bylaw was enacted in 1943 and remained in place until 1961, long after the other major sports had integrated.

THE PIONEER

The first black player to qualify for a PGA Tour card was Charles Sifford. The Charlotte, North Carolina, native had won several tournaments on the nondiscriminatory United Golf Association tour and finally got to showcase his skills against the best competition and for the best prizes when he was 39. Despite being past his prime, Sifford won two PGA events in his career, the Greater Hartford Open in 1967 and the Los Angeles Open in 1969.

THE KING

By the 1960s, many changes were happening throughout the sport. Besides integration, one of the big changes was the influence of television. One of the biggest **beneficiaries** of the medium's association with the game was the "King," Arnold Palmer of Latrobe, Pennsylvania.

Palmer broke in as a rookie in 1955 and won his first major at the Masters in 1958. By 1960, television golf coverage was commonplace, and the **telegenic** Palmer was front and center. He stole the 1960 Masters from Ken Venturi in dramatic fashion over the final two holes as thousands watched. Palmer wore his emotions on his sleeve, and viewers loved it. That year's U.S. Open featured another Palmer comeback win, and the country watched again. His fans started calling themselves "Arnie's Army." In 1962, however, his biggest rival curtailed Palmer's dominance.

THE GOLDEN BEAR

Jack Nicklaus' first year on the PGA Tour was 1962, and the highly touted rookie did not disappoint. He won the U.S. Open in a playoff, defeating Palmer by three shots, making Nicklaus the youngest champion since Bobby Jones. Nicklaus would go on to surpass Palmer and South African star Gary Player as the dominant player of the 1960s and 1970s.

Nicklaus was proficient at hitting the ball long and straight and was a genius at course management. He thought the game extremely well, playing to avoid situations that brought deficiencies in his game into play. Over the years, the tools to help him do that improved. One of the biggest improvements was the introduction of graphite clubs in 1973. Nicklaus went on to build a golf empire, encompassing everything from golf equipment and apparel to wine and golf academies. As one of the greatest players ever, Nicklaus is also highly in demand as a course designer, with more than 300 to his credit.

Twenty-three-year-old Arnold Palmer in the United States Coast Guard in 1953.

Jack Nicklaus at the 2006 Memorial Tournament tees off # 18

Tiger Woods at the Ryder Cup on September 9, 2004, in Bloomfield Hills, Michigan.

MORE GREAT WOMEN

Great players continued to develop on the women's side as well. As Player and Nicklaus dominated the PGA into the 1970s, Nancy Lopez emerged on the LPGA Tour.

Lopez was a golf **prodigy**, winning the New Mexico Women's Amateur at 12. When she joined the LPGA, she won nine tournaments in her first full season, 1978, including one major. This landed Lopez on the cover of *Sports Illustrated* and made her the most recognized name in women's golf. She not only led the tour in prize money and scoring average that season, but she repeated the trick in 1979 as well.

SWEDISH STAR

When Lopez retired in 2002, Swede Annika Sörenstam had established herself as the most dominant player in the game—and perhaps of all time. Sörenstam had been winning majors since her second year on the tour in 1995. Between 1995 and 2006, she won at least two tournaments every year and at least one major every year except 1999 and 2000. In the year she retired, 2008, she won three tournaments.

Sörenstam was so dominant at the turn of the century that she won five straight LPGA Player of the Year awards from 2001 to 2005. Her only real golf rival at the height of her success was Tiger Woods.

TIGER'S TALE

Woods had established himself as the best player in the world by 2000. When he won the 2001 Masters, he became the defending champion in all four majors, a feat known as the Tiger Slam. Similar to Sörenstam, he won at least one major every year from 1999 to 2008, except 2003 and 2004. The two developed a friendly rivalry where they would needle each other by phone or text over who had the most majors. In 2005, she sent Woods a text that simply read "9-9" after winning the LPGA Championship.

Woods had few rivals of his own on the PGA Tour. After changing golf forever with his record-setting 12-shot win at the 1997 Masters, he did what Francis Ouimet had done 84 years earlier, thrust golf into the spotlight, but with 1,000 times the wattage. Wherever Woods played, attendance was at capacity, and TV ratings were at all-time highs, especially for majors.

Tiger Woods changed the game like no one before him ever had, paving the way for the sport's newest stars to step into some very big shoes.

U.S. professional golfer Nancy Lopez.

Annika Sörenstam at the LPGA Championship at Bulle Rock Golf Course, on June 3, 2008 in Havre de Grace, Maryland.

Text-Dependent Questions:

1. Black players were banned from playing on the PGA Tour by a bylaw in its constitution that required all members to be of the Caucasian race. When was this bylaw enacted, and how long was it in practice before being changed?

2. Who was the first black player to qualify for a PGA Tour card?

3. With a win in the 2001 Masters, which golfer became the defending champion in all four majors?

Research Project:

It took the PGA much longer than other organized athletics to achieve integration of black players. Look back at the history of famous black golfers, and chart their major contributions to the sport.

*Bubba Watson chips out of the sand trap
at Hole 5 at the Travelers Championship
at TPC River Highlands Golf Course 2008.*

Words to Understand:

mantle: the position of someone who has responsibility or authority

elude: to fail to be achieved by someone

affinity: a liking for or an attraction to something

CHAPTER  6

MODERN-DAY STARS

Without Charlie Sifford, there may not have been a Tiger Woods. And without Woods, it is impossible to say how many of today's young stars may have ended up pursuing something other than golf. But pursue it they did to ever-amazing results.

MEN

England's Rory McIlroy took the **mantle** from Woods as the best player in the world in 2014. That year, Woods' last stint of 60 weeks at the top of the world rankings ended, and McIlroy took over the top spot for 54 straight weeks when he won the Bridgestone Invitational and the PGA Championship in back-to-back weeks.

The 2014 PGA Championship was McIlroy's fourth major win. He has 11 total PGA tour victories and has been the number one player in the world for more than 90 total weeks. McIlroy is a two-time PGA Player of the Year.

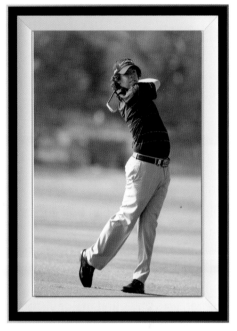

Rory McIlroy playing in the second round of the European Tour European Open golf tournament 2009.

Emerging as McIlroy's biggest rival in 2015, 21-year-old Jordan Spieth won the Masters and the U.S. Open in just his third season. He also finished fourth in the British Open and second in the PGA Championship. The Texan also won the Valspar and the John Deere-sponsored tournaments in 2015, a combination of results that earned him the number one ranking in the world for three weeks.

Spieth has six total tour wins in his career, including the Tour Championship to clinch the FedEx Cup. Spieth was named PGA Player of the Year for 2015 to go along with his 2013 Rookie of the Year award.

Jordan Spieth

Jason Day

Spieth was runner-up in that 2015 PGA Championship to Australian Jason Day. The four-round total of 268 helped Day break a record. A score of 268 is 20 shots under par at Wisconsin's Whistling Straits course, the lowest score versus par for any major champion. The previous record was –19 by Woods at the British Open in 2000.

The win was Day's first major victory and his fifth career win. He had three top 10 finishes in majors in 2015. Before the PGA Championship win, Day had finished in the top 10 at majors nine times, including three runners-up.

Of Day's seven career wins, five came in 2015, including a victory at the Canadian Open. He won by a single stroke over Bubba Watson, a left-handed player who grew up near Pensacola, Florida.

Watson won his first tournament in 2010, and in 2012, he won his first major in dramatic fashion at the 2012 Masters. The tournament came down to a sudden-death playoff with South African Louis Oosthuizen, with Watson saving par from deep in the woods on the second playoff hole to win. He has six other tour wins, including the 2014 Masters.

The tour's most famous left-hander is not Watson. That distinction belongs to Phil Mickelson, a San Diego, California, native with an aggressive style and a brilliant short game. Mickelson already is considered by many to be one of the best players in the sport's history. He certainly has been one of its most popular since joining the tour in 1992.

West of Ireland, Dromoland Golf Course has been described as an experience never to be forgotten, presenting a stern challenge to both professionals and amateurs.

Pebble Beach Golf links, Monterey, California, Hole 8.

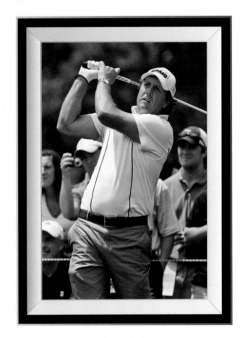

Phil Mickelson

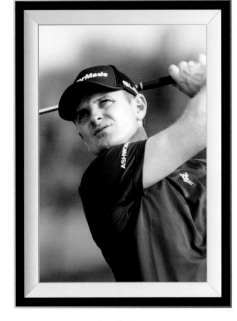

Justin Rose

Mickelson has won 42 PGA tournaments, including five majors. The only major to **elude** him is the U.S. Open, where he has been runner-up six times. At the Masters, he has 15 top 10 finishes, including three wins.

In 2010, Mickelson won the Masters and was fourth in the U.S. Open, but that was not good enough to win PGA Player of the Year. That honor went to Mickelson's longtime Ryder Cup teammate, Jim Furyk. Furyk, who grew up near Philadelphia, won three tournaments that year. That included winning the season-ending playoff tournament, the Tour Championship, to give him the FedEx Cup.

Furyk has 17 career PGA Tour wins, including the 2003 U.S. Open, his only major championship. He nearly has won a second major several times, posting 21 top 10 finishes in majors, including three runners-up.

Englishman Justin Rose, like Furyk, has one major to his credit, winning the U.S. Open in 2013, 10 years after Furyk won his. Rose is 10 years younger than Furyk, so he has more time to get that next major. He has 10 other top 10 major finishes. The closest was at the 2015 Masters, when he was runner-up to a record-tying performance by Justin Spieth.

Rose has six other PGA Tour wins to go along with his U.S. Open title. He plays several European Tour events every year, limiting his opportunities to build his PGA Tour win total.

Germany's Martin Kaymer, like many players from the UK and Europe, also plays a number of European Tour events each season. At the beginning of his career, from 2007 to 2012, he played mainly on the European Tour, playing only a handful of U.S. events. Beginning in 2008, a win at the Abu Dhabi event got him into the Masters, and his high world ranking since has qualified him for all the majors.

Kaymer took full advantage, winning the 2010 PGA Championship and rising to number one in the world for eight weeks in February of 2011. Kaymer also won the 2014 U.S. Open.

WOMEN

On the LPGA Tour, South Korean Inbee Park is the best player. The 2013 LPGA Player of the Year spent 102 weeks ranked number one in the world from 2013 to 2015, ending all three years atop the rankings.

Park has 16 career wins and seven major titles, including three consecutive Women's PGA Championships. In 2008, she became the youngest U.S. Open champion in history at age 19. In 2013 Park won the first three majors of the season, including the ANA Inspiration Tournament, giving her a Career Grand Slam. The Evian was added as a major in 2013.

Park owes a great deal of her success to her pioneer countrywoman, Se Ri Pak. Pak was one of just three South Koreans on the LPGA Tour when she won Rookie of the Year in 1998. When she was inducted into the World Golf Hall of Fame in 2008, there were 45 South Koreans on the tour.

Pak has 25 wins including five majors in her career, but four wins and two of the majors came in her spectacular rookie year. This ignited a golf explosion in South Korea. By 2015, 11 other South Korean women had won majors.

South Koreans would have seen even more success over the years if not for the play of veteran star Cristie Kerr. The Miami, Florida, native joined the tour the year before Pak and has been one of the steadiest players in the world over her long career. Kerr did not win

Inbee Park

Cristie Kerr

her first tournament until 2002 but has since won 16 others, including two majors. South Koreans have been the runners-up on seven occasions.

Kerr was the top-ranked player in the world for five weeks in 2010. Only two players have more career earnings than Kerr's $16 million plus.

Yani Tseng is also one of the top 15 leaders in career earnings. For two years, the Chinese star was almost unbeatable on the LPGA Tour. Between April of 2010 and March of 2012, Tseng won 13 tournaments, including four majors. She was ranked number one in the world for 109 consecutive weeks.

Tseng won the 2008 LPGA Rookie of the Year award when she won the first of her five total majors. Tseng is a two-time LPGA Player of the Year winner. She is the fastest player in tour history to reach $2 million in career earnings.

The explosion of Asian talent on the LPGA Tour has made it challenging for homegrown American players to break through, but Ohio's Stacy Lewis has had excellent results in her brilliant career. Lewis was the top-ranked player in the world for five months in 2014, the year she claimed 3 of her 11 career wins and was the tour's money leader and Player of the Year.

Stacy Lewis

Paula Creamer

Lewis also won Player of the Year in 2012, when she won four tournaments. A four-year All-American at Arkansas, Lewis also has two major victories since her LPGA debut in 2009.

Although a year younger than Lewis, Californian Paula Creamer had eight LPGA Tour victories under her belt by 2009. Creamer qualified for her tour card just four months after turning 18. In her rookie season of 2005, she won twice, capturing Rookie of the Year honors. Creamer won four tournaments in 2008, and in 2010 won her first major at the U.S. Women's Open.

Creamer has 14 top 10 finishes in major tournaments. Dubbed the Pink Panther due to her **affinity** for wearing the color on the course, Creamer has earned more than $11 million in her career, top 10 all-time.

Another of the tour's American stars is Floridian Lexi Thompson. Thompson made her name in golf circles in 2007 when she qualified for the Women's U.S. Open at age 12. She turned pro at 15 and won her first tournament in 2011 at age 16. The win allowed her to petition for a waiver to the LPGA rule requiring members to be 18, and she was given a tour card for 2012.

Lexi Thompson

Thompson did not win in her rookie season but made up for that with two wins in 2013 along with her first major victory at the 2014 Kraft Nabisco Championship.

One of the tour's veteran stars, Norwegian Suzann Pettersen debuted on the Ladies European Tour in 2001 and won Rookie of the Year. She jumped to the LPGA Tour in 2003, where she struggled to match her European Tour success for the first few years. In 2007, however, Pettersen found her game, winning five tournaments, including her first major, the 2007 LPGA Championship.

In 2013, Pettersen was the inaugural winner of the tour's fifth major, the Evian Championship. She has been close in several majors, with 19 other top 10 finishes, including six runners-up. She has earned more than $13 million in her career.

Text-Dependent Questions:

1. Who is known as the tour's most famous left-hander and winner of 42 PGA tournaments, including five majors?

2. What country is the LPGA Tour's best player from?

3. Who is dubbed the Pink Panther due to her affinity for wearing the color pink on the course?

Research Project:

How is the opportunity in golf different for men and women? Research online the amount of college scholarships available for both men and women in this sport as well as winning purses for various tournaments. Is it a fair playing ground?

SAM SNEAD

TOM WATSON

GARY PLAYER

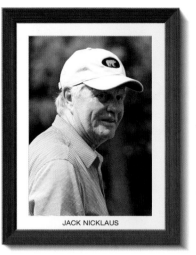

JACK NICKLAUS

BEN HOGAN

ANNIKA SÖRENSTAM

BABE ZAHARIAS (RIGHT)

TIGER WOODS   BOBBY JONES   JULI INKSTER

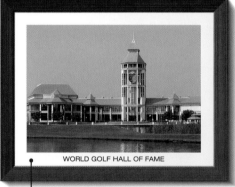

WORLD GOLF HALL OF FAME

LOUISE SUGGS

ARNOLD PALMER

The World Golf Hall of Fame is located just outside St. Augustine, Florida. It has been the sole location since 1998, after incorporating the LPGA Tour Hall of Fame, which had been located in Augusta, Georgia. There are four categories of members: Male Competitor, Female Competitor, Veterans, and Lifetime Achievement. To be eligible, players must be at least 40 years old, have at least 15 tournament wins, including at least two major tournament wins. Eligible players must be named on 75 percent of ballots to be elected. The hall has more than 150 members and gets an average of 350,000 visitors each year.

Scan here to go to the Golf Hall of Fame website.

CHAPTER 7

GOLF'S GREATEST PLAYERS

Jack Nicklaus or Tiger Woods—Tiger Woods or Jack Nicklaus? Which one of these golfers is the best ever to play? Few will dispute that the debate comes down to just these two. Until 2010, it didn't look like it would be a debate at all as Woods had won 71 PGA tournaments and 14 majors in just 14 full seasons. At just 34 years old, it looked like he would cruise past Nicklaus's 18 career major wins and 73 tour victories.

Then Woods' marriage fell apart in late 2009 in a very public fashion, and his game went completely off the rails. He did not win a tournament at all in 2010 or 2011. He recovered in 2012 and by 2013 was back to number one in the world, staying there for 60 weeks. But the wheels came off again in 2014 after a back injury forced surgery. He played only 16 events in 2014 and 2015, missing the cut six times. Since the 2010 season, he has just eight wins, none of them at majors. Now in his 40s, there are questions about whether Woods can ever win on the tour again.

What Woods needs is to be like Nicklaus, who won five tournaments, including three majors after his 40th birthday. Nicklaus was a model of consistency throughout his career, winning at least two tournaments every season from 1962 to 1978. He was as steady as a rock.

Woods was more of a rock star. The way he won tournaments, big tournaments, had literally never been seen before. At 21, he won his very first Masters by shooting a record 18 under par, but more impressively, he won by 12 shots. At the 2000 U.S. Open, he ran away from the field, making it look like he was playing a completely different golf course when he won by 15 shots. He was so powerful off the tee when he was dominating the tour that golf courses sought to make their designs "Tiger-proof," narrowing fairways and lengthening holes to neutralize his power.

No one ever had to "Jack-proof" a course, but Nicklaus just kept winning big tournaments anyway, more than anyone else. Who is better? That should continue to be a great debate topic well into this century.

MEN

There is perhaps no name as synonymous with American golf as Jack Nicklaus. The Golden Bear was not only great, but he also shined in the clutch. Almost 20 percent of his career PGA wins came in playoffs. Another 22 percent were won by a single stroke.

Nicklaus was awarded the Presidential Medal of Freedom in 2005 and a PGA Lifetime Achievement award in 2008. The Presidential Medal of Freedom is the highest civilian award in the United States, given to Nicklaus for "meritorious contribution to . . . significant private or public endeavors." By 2015, only seven players had won a Lifetime Achievement award. It is given for outstanding contributions to the PGA Tour. Nicklaus certainly has made several of those.

Jack Nicklaus

By the numbers, Tiger Woods's career is brilliant. He is second all-time in both career PGA wins and career major tournament wins. Only he and Nicklaus have won each major tournament at least three times. Woods was the Rookie of the Year in 1996 and once won five straight PGA Player of the Year awards. He is also a two-time FedEx Cup Champion.

Growing up in Orange County, California, golf greatness seemed predestined for Woods. Before his third birthday he was putting on a national late-night TV show. By age 12, he could break 70. It has been a fascinating career, one watched by more people than any other player in history.

Tiger Woods

Both Nicklaus and Woods have said that the best swing they ever saw belonged o Ben Hogan. They are just two of the great majority of experts who believe Hogan had the sweetest swing in the game. Hogan used that perfect swing to help him win the Career Grand Slam, accomplished by only four other men.

Hogan had his best season in 1953, when he became the only golfer to ever win the Masters, U.S. Open, and British Open in the same year. This "Triple Crown" feat was so remarkable that a ticker-tape parade was held for him in New York City. The Ben Hogan Award is given annually to the best college golfer in America.

Had it existed when he was at Georgia Tech in the early 1920s, Bobby Jones would easily have won the Ben Hogan Award. Jones went on to become inarguably the best amateur golfer ever as he never turned pro.

As an amateur, Jones regularly beat the professionals he competed against. He won the 1927 Southern Open and the 1930 Southeastern Open, both professional tournaments. His best and last season was 1930, when he also won the U.S. and British Amateurs and the U.S. and British Opens, all considered majors at the time. No other player ever has won four major tournaments in one year. Jones won the U.S. Amateur on four other occasions as well.

Ben Hogan

Bobby Jones

Walter Hagen   *Byron Nelson*

Where Jones was the model amateur, Rochester, NY native Walter Hagen was the template for the early 20th-century pro golfer. While Jones never got paid for golfing, Hagen excelled at it. He made a lot of money playing outside the tour, but he also made his fair share on the tour as well.

Only Nicklaus and Woods have more career major wins than Hagen. He won all of the modern majors at least twice, except the Masters, which he never won. The Masters did not exist until1934 and was not significant until Gene Sarazen made it famous in 1935. Hagen played the Masters just once near the end of his career in 1936, finishing 11th.

Byron Nelson first played the Masters in 1935, finishing ninth. In 1937 he won the event, claiming his first major. In 1945, the Texan had his greatest year on tour and perhaps the greatest year any player has ever had on the PGA Tour. Nelson set two records that year that still stand today. He won an astonishing 18 tournaments in 35 starts, and he won 11 of those tournaments in a row.

Nelson held a record on the tour that stood for more than 50 years. In one stretch of his career, Nelson made 113 consecutive cuts. Only Woods, at 142 in a row, has done better. Nelson is a PGA Tour Lifetime Achievement Award recipient.

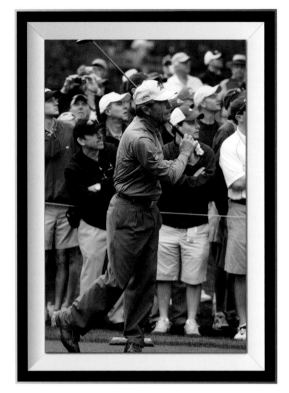

Sam Snead   *Gary Player*

Sam Snead was the fourth PGA Lifetime Achievement Award recipient, receiving the honor in 1998, the year after Nelson. Snead competed regularly against Nelson as they debuted on the tour one year apart, and their careers overlapped for 14 years.

Snead had one of the longest careers in the game's history, playing more than 30 seasons on the tour. He put those years to good use, winning more tournaments than any other player in PGA history. Snead is one of five players to win each of the major tournaments in his career. He played competitively until he was 75, even making the cut at the U.S. Open at age 61.

Gary Player was given a PGA Tour Lifetime Achievement Award in 2012. The South African star was the first non-American to be honored. Only three players won more majors in their careers than Player. He is one of the five players to have achieved a Career Grand Slam, which came with his U.S. Open win in 1965.

Player preached health and fitness throughout his career and was able to play competitively into his 60s. He called for mandatory drug testing on all professional tours. Player made the cut at the 1998 Masters at age 62, a tournament he has played more than 50 times. A renowned course designer, he has designed more than 300 courses around the world.

Along with Player and Nicklaus, Arnold Palmer was the other member of "the Big Three," the trio that dominated the game primarily in the 1960s. Palmer, the oldest of the group, already had four major wins by the time Nicklaus debuted in 1962 and collected two more in that 1962 season.

In 1960, Palmer was credited with establishing the modern Grand Slam. He opened the season by winning the Masters and the U.S. Open and stated to a reporter on the flight over to the UK that if he could win the British Open and the PGA Championship, that would be a Grand Slam. The reporter printed it, and it stuck.

As the dominance of "the Big Three" waned along with the 1970s, Tom Watson rose to fill the void they left. Between 1977 and 1982, the Kansas City, Missouri, native beat Nicklaus in four majors, including twice at the Masters. Watson was a constant threat at the big tournaments throughout his career, racking up 46 top 10 finishes in majors, including eight runners-up.

The one major that Watson never could solve was the PGA Championship. The closest he came was in the 1978 tournament. It was a particularly painful loss as Watson blew a five-shot lead to start the round and lost in a play-off. Only Woods has won more Player of the Year awards than Watson.

Tom Watson

Arnold Palmer

Career Snapshots

BOBBY JONES 1920–30

9 PGA wins
7 majors
2-time Walker Cup captain

SAM SNEAD 1931–87

82 PGA wins
7 majors
1949 PGA Player of the Year

WALTER HAGEN 1912–40

45 PGA wins
11 majors
6-time Ryder Cup captain

JACK NICKLAUS 1961–2005

73 PGA wins
18 majors
5-time PGA Player of the Year

BYRON NELSON 1932–46

52 PGA wins
5 majors
2-time AP Male Athlete of the Year

ARNOLD PALMER 1954–2006

62 PGA wins
7 majors
2-time PGA Player of the Year

BEN HOGAN 1930–71

64 PGA wins
9 majors
4-time PGA Player of the Year

GARY PLAYER 1957–2009

24 PGA wins
9 majors
1961 PGA Tour money leader

All the above athletes are members of the Hall of Fame with the exception of current players.

TOM WATSON 1971–Present

39 PGA wins
8 majors
6-time PGA Player of the Year

TIGER WOODS 1996–Present

79 PGA wins
14 majors
11-time PGA Player of the Year

WOMEN

In the women's game, the most prolific player the sport has seen is Sweden's Annika Sörenstam. She was so good that she even tried her hand at the men's game. In 2003 Sörenstam played in the PGA's Colonial Tournament. She drove well but putted poorly and missed the cut. That almost never happened to Sörenstam on the LPGA Tour.

In 57 career major appearances, Sörenstam missed the cut just four times. She made 24 cuts in a row at one stretch and finished in the top ten 31 times. In her 18-year career, Sörenstam made 298 of 307 cuts, or 97 percent of them. She is the leader on the LPGA career money list, with more than $22 million won.

Kathy Whitworth is the leader on the LPGA career tournament wins list. The Texas legend debuted on the LPGA Tour in 1958 and won her first tournament in 1962. From there, she never looked back, winning at least one tournament every season from 1962 to 1978, a record streak.

Annika Sörenstam

Whitworth could have won even more if she was better at playoffs, going 8–20 in her career. But overall the wins were plentiful, the most of any PGA professional, man or woman. She was the first woman to reach $1 million in career earnings. Whitworth also led the LPGA Tour in scoring average a record seven times. She missed a Career Grand Slam as she never won the U.S. Open.

The only other woman with more career wins that Sörenstam is Mickey Wright. Like Sörenstam, Wright is one of six players to win the LPGA Career Grand Slam. Wright, born in San Diego in 1935, joined the PGA Tour in 1955. She won her first tournament the following year at the Jacksonville Open.

Only one woman has won more majors than Wright, who won her first at the 1958 LPGA Championship. She won at least one major tournament in seven consecutive seasons from 1958 to 1964. In that stretch, she led the tour in scoring average for five straight years, 1960 to 1964. Sweet-swinging Ben Hogan himself once said Wright's swing was the best he ever saw.

Babe Didrikson Zaharias was one of the best athletes anyone ever saw. The Associated Press called the multisport star the ninth-greatest athlete of the 20th century and the Woman Athlete of the 20th Century.

As a golfer, Zaharias is top 10 all-time in LPGA career wins and top 5 all-time in career major tournaments won. She would have ranked higher had cancer not cut her life short at 45. She won a major as recently as 1954, two years before her death. That was also the year she won her last Associated Press Female Athlete of the Year award. Zaharias is the only woman to make the cut in a PGA event, which she did three times.

Zaharias and Patty Berg were not only cofounders of the LPGA but were the tour's two best players as well. Berg not only won more majors than anyone in history; she has the fifth-most LPGA tournament wins as well. Three of her wins in majors came with Berg playing as an amateur.

Berg turned pro in 1940 at age 22 but put her career on hold to serve in the military as a recruitment officer. Between when she returned to the tour in1945 and 1958, she won at least one tournament every year. In 1946, she was the winner of the inaugural U.S. Women's Open. She led the tour in scoring average three times in the 1950s.

Babe Didrikson Zaharias

Patty Berg

Nancy Lopez

Louise Suggs

In 1957, the year Berg won two majors in a season for the third time, Nancy Lopez was born near Los Angeles. Like Berg, Lopez made a major impact on women's golf. Lopez's LPGA Rookie of the Year-winning 1978 season gained national attention. She had five consecutive wins and nine overall, the best rookie season ever for a man or woman.

After Lopez, money and fans both increased for the LPGA. Prize money jumped to a total of more than $4 million in 1979, and crowds tripled. Lopez's gallery dubbed themselves "Nancy's Navy," with a wink to Arnold Palmer fans. Success in majors was elusive for Lopez, although she did win the LPGA Championship three times.

The Rookie of the Year award Lopez won in 1978 is named for Louise Suggs, an Atlanta native and one of the original members of the LPGA. Her pro career began in 1948. Suggs has the fourth-most career LPGA wins and the third-most major tournament wins in tour history.

Suggs retired in 1962 but continued to receive honors in the sport throughout her life. In 2007, she received the Bob Jones award from the USGA for "distinguished sportsmanship in golf." Six months before her death in 2015, she was one of seven women granted membership at the revered Royal and Ancient Golf Club of St. Andrew's, previously an all-male club.

Karrie Webb

Juli Inkster

Another winner of the Louise Suggs Rookie of the Year award is Karrie Webb. The Australian won in 1996 and went on to have one of the most successful careers in golf. She has earned nearly $20 million in career winnings, second only to Sörenstam.

Webb's 1996 season included four wins, and she would win multiple tournaments for each of the next six seasons, including six of her major tournament wins. She also led the league in scoring average three times in that stretch. Webb is the only player in history to achieve the Super Career Grand Slam, winning five different LPGA major tournaments. She is top 10 in both career LPGA wins and majors won.

Juli Inkster won Rookie of the Year a dozen years before Webb in 1984. The Santa Cruz, California, native charged out of the gate with two wins that year—but not just any two. She won the Dinah Shore and the du Maurier Classic, both majors at the time. Inkster went on to win both the U.S. Open and the LPGA Championship in 1999 to complete the Career Grand Slam.

Inkster is in the top 10 on the career major tournament wins list and in the top 20 for career wins. She also had 23 other top 10 finishes in majors. Inkster has said that her best accomplishment as a golfer is winning three straight Women's U.S. Amateur Titles.

Betsy Rawls never played in the Women's U.S. Amateur, but the University of Texas Longhorn played and won back-to-back Texas Amateur titles in 1949 and 1950, remarkable for a player who did not take up the game until age 17. Rawls went on to a pro career in 1951, one that ended 25 years later with her in the top 10 in LPGA tournaments and majors won. In 1959, she won 10 events and led the tour in wins on three occasions.

Rawls won at least one tournament for 15 straight seasons, a streak second only to Whitworth's 17. Following her career, Rawls received the Patty Berg award for "exemplifying diplomacy, sportsmanship, goodwill, and contributions to the game of golf." She also received the Bob Jones award in 1996.

Career Snapshots

BABE ZAHARIAS 1947–56

41 LPGA wins

10 majors

5-time AP Female Athlete of the Year

PATTY BERG 1940–62

60 LPGA wins

15 majors

3-time AP Female Athlete of the Year

LOUISE SUGGS 1948–62

61 LPGA wins

11 majors

2-time LPGA Tour money leader

MICKEY WRIGHT 1955–69

82 LPGA wins

13 majors

2-time AP Female Athlete of the Year

BETSY RAWLS 1951–75

55 LPGA wins

8 majors

2-time LPGA Tour money leader

KATHY WHITWORTH 1958–2005

88 LPGA wins

6 majors

7-time LPGA Player of the Year

NANCY LOPEZ 1978–2008

48 LPGA wins

3 majors

4-time LPGA Player of the Year

ANNIKA SÖRENSTAM 1993–2008

72 LPGA wins

10 majors

8-time LPGA Player of the Year

JULI INKSTER 1983– Present

31 LPGA wins

7 majors

2015 Solheim Cup captain

KARRIE WEBB 1996– Present

41 LPGA wins

7 majors

2-time LPGA Player of the Year

All the above athletes are members of the Hall of Fame.

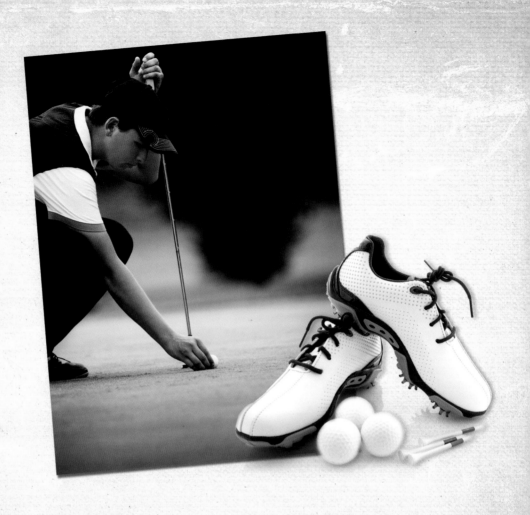

 Words to Understand:

affluence: abundance of money, property, and other material goods; riches; wealth

entrenched: to place in a position of strength; establish firmly or solidly

prodigious: wonderful or marvelous

CHAPTER  8

THE FUTURE OF GOLF

Dealing with a sport as old as golf that has changed as little as it has over the decades, it is difficult to project any big changes in the future. Equipment gets better, players get stronger, but the game stays the same.

WHO'S PLAYING?

Although the game itself has not changed very much, the number of people playing it has. From 2010 to 2014, golf participation fell, especially among young adults 18 to 34, and for eight straight years, more courses closed than opened in the United States. This decline was not seen across the board in this age group for sports in general. Their participation rate in sports was up 29 percent. Golf has an image problem in the United States.

The Kawana Fuji course (ranked 80th in the world) is often called Japan's Pebble Beach because it is a golf resort set on cliffs near the ocean.

Japan's Chie Arimura waiting for her turn during HSBC Women's Champions at the Sensota Golf Club Serapong Course in Singapore.

Michelle Wie, of the United States, participates in the Honda LPGA Thailand at the Siam Country Club Pattaya Old Course in Chonburi, Thailand.

In markets like Asia, the game is thriving in no small part due to the success of players from that region on the tour, especially on the women's side. After peaking in the United States at 30 million players in 2003, however, the decline began, falling to about 25 million in 2014. Golf is relatively slow and expensive to play. A round takes four hours, a block of time this generation rarely devotes to anything other than sleep and especially when the payoff is not immediate. The sport also is associated with **affluence** and exclusivity. Golf has a long history of not being inclusive, which has not endeared it to a generation that values diversity and equality. So in 2014, the USGA initiated Play 9, a campaign designed to encourage young people who might not want to commit the time or money to 18 holes to get out and play 9 instead. The campaign uses young stars like the popular U.S. Open Champion Michelle Wie to get its message out in the hope of bringing a new generation to the game in the future.

THE OLYMPIC GAME

In 2016, golf became an Olympic sport again for the first time since 1904. It will be interesting to see if this kind of international exposure creates new fans or reinforces the **entrenched** notions that already exist. In markets like the UK, Australia, and Japan, former golf hotbeds, the game is on the decline. Golf participation in England is down 25 percent since 2007. In Australia, club memberships are down 20 percent since 1998, and in Japan, participation is down 40 percent since the early 1990s.

Some markets in continental Europe like Germany and the Czech Republic have seen interest in the sport grow, but the hope is that a worldwide TV audience will raise golf's profile and build on the interest in places like Latin America and Asia, where the game has prospered recently.

The St. Andrews 2000 Golf Club, located 75 miles (120 km) southeast of Bangkok, Thailand.

Karlstejn Golf Resort in Czech Republic.

Gormanstown College Golf Club in Ireland.

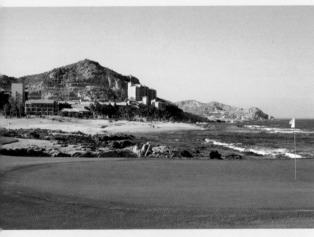

Cabo Del Sol Golf Course in Mexico.

Dubai Creek Golf & Yacht Club in Dubai.

The Royal Bangkok Sports Club in Thailand.

La Quinta Golf Course in Spain.

PREDICTIONS

To encourage growth of the sport, there are a number of things around the game itself that will have to change as society does:

- Golf must be more family friendly. The days when fathers can escape to the links leaving weekend parenting to equally stressed-out wives are in the past. Dads spend time with their kids on the weekend, so the golf course needs to be somewhere that can happen.

- Golf must embrace women. Women are taking up golf at a faster rate than men. Courses built for long hitters or clubs that exclude female members will find themselves in the rough.

- Golf must embrace technology. Smartphone apps that help with club decisions and sensor-equipped clubs are being developed to make the game easier to manage. Improved golf simulation technology can keep players in cold-weather regions golfing year round.

- Golf must complement traditional courses with options. Six- and nine-hole formats will lower the bar of entry for new players.

Kids practicing with a trainer.

A player keeping score on a mobile GPS device next to the green.

FUTURE STARS

LYDIA KO

To call New Zealander Lydia Ko a child prodigy would be to sell her short. Her brief career is not just **prodigious** but also unprecedented in a spectacular way. Ko won her first pro tournament as an amateur in 2012 at 14 years old, the youngest pro tournament winner ever, male or female. She won another pro tournament in 2013 before turning pro at 16. In her rookie 2014 season, she won three times to capture LPGA Rookie of the Year. In 2015, she added four more wins, including her first major at the Evian Championship and was briefly ranked number one in the world at 17.

Lydia Ko of New Zealand won the LPGA Canadian Pacific Women's Open golf tournament at the Vancouver Golf Club in Coquitlam, Canada, Aug. 23, 2015.

JUSTIN THOMAS

In 2015, PGA rookie Justin Thomas made 23 of 30 cuts and had 15 top 25 finishes, including seven top 10 finishes. The Louisville, Kentucky, native had a stellar college career at the University of Alabama, where he was named most outstanding collegiate golfer in 2012 and won the National Collegiate Athletic Association (NCAA) Team Championship in 2013.

BRYSON DECHAMBEAU

Southern Methodist University (SMU) star and California native Bryson DeChambeau joined some very exclusive company in 2015. That season, his senior year at SMU, DeChambeau won the NCAA title then capped the year by winning the U.S. Amateur as well. Only four other golfers ever have accomplished this double in the same year: Nicklaus, Mickelson, Woods, and Ryan Moore. DeChambeau was one of the top ranked amateurs in the world and beat a very strong international field to win the U.S. Amateur title.

THE 19TH HOLE

These players will have careers that see more competitors from current nontraditional markets and grow using technology that is only now being developed. The centuries-old game of hitting the ball from tee to cup remains the same, but to thrive again in America, it will need to look a lot different in decades to come.

Text-Dependent Questions:

1. Name some reasons why the game of golf has declined in America in recent years.

2. In 2016, golf became an Olympic sport again for the first time since which year?

3. Which up-and-coming star is known as the youngest pro tournament winner ever, male or female?

Research Project:

What kind of technology is being developed or predicted for the future that will enhance the game of golf? Is the United States or are other countries leading the research?

GLOSSARY OF GOLF TERMS

ace: a hole in one.

away: the golfer who plays first following the tee shot. His or her ball lies farthest from the hole.

birdie: a hole a player completes in one stroke less than par; for example, he or she uses three strokes to finish a par 4 hole.

bogey: a hole a player completes in one stroke more than the par, for example, he or she uses four strokes to finish a par 3 hole. Each stroke above has its own name: two strokes above is a double bogey, three strokes is a triple bogey, and so on.

bunker: low areas filled with sand along the fairways and around the greens. They make the holes more difficult.

caddy: a player's assistant who carries the clubs and gives advice on how to play the hole.

cut: the group of best golfers in a tournament. Most of the time, a few less than half of the players in the lead after two rounds of play compete in the final rounds. The rest are eliminated.

draw: a shot made with sidespin on purpose or on accident. For a right-handed player, it causes the ball to drift from right to left. The opposite is a fade.

eagle: a hole a player completes in two strokes less than par, such as finishing a par 5 in three strokes. Three strokes below par is a double eagle, also known as an "albatross."

fade: a shot made with a spin, usually on purpose, that makes the ball drift from left to right for a right-handed golfer. The opposite is a draw.

fairway: the long, sometimes narrow lane of short grass where the golfer aims from the tee. Most of the time, the fairway is the best place from which to take the second shot.

flag: the brightly colored banner that marks the hole. It is taken out once players are on the green.

front and back nine: the course's first nine holes are the front, and the last nine are the back.

Grand Slam: winning all four of golf's major tournaments in the same calendar year. No golfer has ever won a modem Grand Slam: the Masters, the U.S. Open, the British Open, and the PGA Championship.

green: the close-cut area of grass where the hole is located. Once the players have reached the green, they try to putt the ball around mounds and curves into the hole.

handicap: a measure of a player's skill level. A player who averages 77 strokes on a par 73 course has a 4 handicap (77 − 73 = 4). More difficult courses change handicaps.

hole: where the players aim on a golf course, just 4¼ inches (10.8 cm) in diameter and 4 inches (10.2 cm) deep. Typically there are 18 holes, although smaller courses may have 9. A flag marks the holes to help players see it from a distance.

hook: a bad shot that, for a right-handed golfer, goes drastically from right to left. The opposite is a slice.

lie: the positioning of a ball on the ground. A good lie means the ball is on flat area; a bad lie might be in the rough or in a sand trap.

out and back: courses that are farthest away from the end at the 9th hole and return at the end of the 18th hole.

par: the standard number of strokes to complete a hole or course or when a player finishes a hole in the standard number of strokes.

penalty: strokes added to the score if the player loses a ball, hits the ball into a water hazard, or commits another infraction.

rough: the thick, grassy areas bordering the fairway and greens.

round: completing the course. A player who uses 78 strokes to finish an 18-hole course has a round of 78.

short game: the skills a player uses near and on the greens: chipping, escaping bunkers, and putting.

slice: a bad shot that, for a right-handed golfer, curves drastically from left to right. The opposite is a hook.

stroke play: the most common method of scoring in golf. The winner has the lowest number of strokes.

tee shot: the first shot at the hole, taken from the tee box. The player places the ball on a small wood or plastic peg placed in the ground. The player who scored better on the previous hole plays first.

tour: a series of tournaments, usually based on player skill or regions. The most prestigious are the PGA Tour in the United States and the European PGA Tour.

water hazards: areas on the golf course covered by water. When a shot falls into the water, the player can play it if he or she can find it, but if the ball is lost, the player gets a one-stroke penalty.

yardage: the distance from the tee, or the player's position on a hole, to the flag. Men's tees are farther back than women's tees. To determine course yardage (usually between 6,500 and 7,000 yards [5,950 m and 6,400 m]), the yardage for each hole is added together.

CHRONOLOGY

1457 James II of Scotland bans golf in the interest of national defense.

1834 William II confers the titles of "royal" and "ancient" upon the golf club of St. Andrews.

1848 Introduction of the gutta percha ball.

1861 First British Open held and won by Old Tom Morris.

1888 Formation of the first U.S. golf club, St. Andrew's at Yonkers, New York.

1894 USGA is formed.

1901 Rubber-cored golf ball is invented.

1913 Francis Ouimet, at 21 years old, defeats Vardon and Ray in the U.S. Open, popularizing golf in America.

1927 U.S. team defeats Britain in inaugural Ryder Cup match.

1930 Bobby Jones scores a grand slam, winning the U.S. and British Opens and Amateurs in the same year.

1932 USGA approves the 1.68-inch (4.3 cm) diameter golf ball, making it the standard.

1949 LPGA is formed.

1953 First nationally televised golf tournament airs.

1963 Arnold Palmer becomes the first golfer to win more than $100,000 in one year. Jack Nicklaus wins his first Masters and for 17 years holds the record of being youngest person to do so.

1975 Lee Elder becomes the first African American invited to play at the Masters.

1986 Official World Golf Rankings established.

1986 Jack Nicklaus wins his sixth Masters; at age 46 he becomes the oldest player to do it.

1990 The Solheim Cup is introduced, pitting professional women golfers from the United States against those from Europe.

1997 Tiger Woods, at 21, becomes the youngest to win the Masters Tournament; Woods sets a Masters record of 270.

2002 Suzy Whaley, an LPGA and PGA professional, becomes the first woman to qualify for a PGA Tour event—the 2003 Greater Hartford Open.

2002 Rich Beem makes equipment history at the PGA Championship, becoming the first player to claim one of golf's four major championships with a set of graphite shafts.

2003 Michelle Wie, age 13, becomes the youngest woman to win a USGA adult women's competition: the U.S. Women's Amateur Public Links Championship in Palm Coast, Florida.

2014 The Royal and Ancient Golf Club of St. Andrew's Scotland approves a motion to admit women members.

2014 Tiger Woods sets the record for most time spent as the world's top-ranked player.

Golf Today: Golf returned as a medal sport at the 2016 Summer Olympic Games in Brazil for the first time since 1904. 60 men and 60 women qualified for their respective 72-hole events. Both players and IGF officials lobbied to have their sport included once again in the world's premier sporting event.

FURTHER READING

Young, Jeff. *Michelle Wie (Extreme Athletes)*. Greensboro, NC: Morgan Reynolds Publishing, 2011

Uschan, Michael V. *Golf (Science Behind Sports)*. Independence, KY: Lucent Books, 2015

Hasday, Judy. *Tiger Woods: Athlete (Black Americans of Achievement)*. Broomall, PA: Chelsea House Publishing, 2008

INTERNET RESOURCES:

Professional Golfers Association http://www.pga.com/home/

Ladies Professional Golfers Association http://www.lpga.com/

Golf Magazine http://www.golf.com/

World Golf Hall of Fame http://www.worldgolfhalloffame.org/

VIDEO CREDITS:

The Double Eagle (pg 8) https://www.youtube.com/watch?v=t2kDdTDM2kg

Miracle at Merion (pg 9) https://www.youtube.com/watch?v=naiAcCoTgsE

Palmer's Comeback (pg 10) https://www.youtube.com/watch?v=XjN1r2mLtDU

The Golden Bear Wins His Sixth (pg 11) https://www.youtube.com/watch?v=STb0KZFox8w

Mize's Masterful Chip (pg 12) https://www.youtube.com/watch?v=NvQa4fbETKU

"The Greatest Performance in Golf History" (pg 13) https://www.youtube.com/watch?v=FJM3iOvoVLQ

Birdie for Birdie (pg 14) https://www.youtube.com/watch?v=2aKjBhtAxJc

Bubba Golf (pg 15) https://www.youtube.com/watch?v=W00lrCnG-B8

QR CODES AND LINKS TO THIRD-PARTY CONTENT

You may gain access to certain third-party content ("Third-Party Sites") by scanning and using the QR Codes that appear in this publication (the "QR Codes"). We do not operate or control in any respect any information, products, or services on such Third-Party Sites linked to by us via the QR Codes included in this publication, and we assume no responsibility for any materials you may access using the QR Codes. Your use of the QR Codes may be subject to terms, limitations, or restrictions set forth in the applicable terms of use or otherwise established by the owners of the Third-Party Sites. Our linking to such Third-Party Sites via the QR Codes does not imply an endorsement or sponsorship of such Third-Party Sites, or the information, products, or services offered on or through the Third- Party Sites, nor does it imply an endorsement or sponsorship of this publication by the owners of such Third-Party Sites.

PICTURE CREDITS

INDEX

In this index, page numbers in **bold italics** font indicate photos or videos.